WHY DO WE NEED A FRIEND

OUR SUPPORT SYSTEM

SHUBHAM GUPTA

XpressPublishing

An imprint of Notion Press

No.8, 3rd Cross Street,CIT Colony,
Mylapore, Chennai, Tamil Nadu-600004

ISBN 978-1-64919-678-1

I WANT TO DEDICATE THIS BOOK TO
MY BEST FRIENDS BITTU, ANIL AND
PRAMOD

Contents

Foreword

THIS BOOK IS ALL ABOUT WHY DO WE NEED A FRIEND IN OUR LIFE.

Acknowledgements

I WOULD LIKE TO THANK SOME OF MY
FRIENDS FOR HELPING ME WHILE WRITING
THIS BOOK. AND I WOULD ALSO LIKE TO
THANKS MY PARENTS AND TEACHERS
WHO MADE ME ABLE TO WRITE A BOOK

CHAPTER ONE

LIFE

Life gives you a reason to smile, we should enjoy our life to the fullest because we only get one life . we should live like that life because we only get life once . one life is enough to fulfill our dreams , to be happy. One purpose of life is to be happy and make others happy too. And this life will show us many colors , sometimes this will give you sadness too . so do not fed up with this . sadness, happiness all our part of life . learn to fight with every situation of life . do what makes you feel happy. Live the life of our dreams because dreams are what we are having for . be brave enough to live the life of your dreams according to your vision not in the opinion of others. People will sometimes gives you lot of stress into your happy life . so never be stressed, believe in yourself to live life like your own . you should only keep looking up, that's the most powerful thing of life. Life is life which we live , we enjoy, we celebrate, we are sometimes happy, sometimes sad , but still we want to live . some people face very much difficulties in life and some people are born with silver spoon . some struggle in their life to fulfill their dreams and some have to order only what they want . some do not even get basic necessities like food, clothes and shelter. Some are so rich that they can purchase anything and in between rich and poor there exists the middle class . middle class people are those people who keep a lot of balance in their life having a limited income not very high savings and having lot of plans for their future . according to me life is a festival of happiness . we should have to celebrate it daily, sometimes life can surprise us with happy coincidences . life is a mixture of everything we do from our birth to end . some people think that only earning is life or only living it like a pro is , finding a good job, marrying a good partner, coming into relationships , travelling. But it is nothing like that for me . for me life is only complete when my family is with me because I am grown up in a joint family and I know very well the importance of family in our life. Family is the only place where you get the unconditional love which we go and find from others . we cannot get everything in one life because we are human beings and we are not ever satisfied with what we have , we always want something extra from what we have . expectations of human beings are always very high . I think we have to stay happy in our life , stay connected to our social surrounding as human being is a social animal.

CHAPTER TWO

A FRIEND

What actually a friend is? Merely a person whom we meet on some sort of social platform or somewhere we go daily . no not at all, it is the one whom we feel our space with, the one we are comfortable with and the one whose thinking intends to match with ours . friend can be the sole which shows immortal love and inculcate the lacking trust which the unhonoured world tries to snatch from us with each passing day .

Friends are needed because they are the pillars at which when our this little body gets a weary of the great world tends to rest upon. The pillar which provides us the back support when we are in a thirsty need of it . friends are the one which prevents us to get into the state of want wit sadness by some entertainment or to the extremest wich they can do. Some friends are so special that they always stand in the eye of honour, they make everyday special just by being themselves . sometimes when we get this combobulated in certain situations they take us out from it . they stop us to get mesmerized in wrong activities which someday might have made us retent they are the one with whom, whenever neded , we can have insanc conversations which often help us to keep ourselves in the state of euphoria they are the one who's purse, who's person, whose highest means lies all unlocked to us whenever needed .

I would like to reiterate my point that friends are the pillars with which gods hands ahs blessed all. Friends are the threshold of the doors to life through which all have to pass with a charming smile and love so basically, friendship is the loveliest thing which always helps us to gain morality of life and therefore friends are needed to have happiness in abundance. This is the reason they always say that friend are like stars , they will not always be there but you know that they are there.

You need someone to lay your shoulder on and cry (apart from your parents and siblings, to enjoy your life to give suggestions regarding movies, outfits, etc. you need someone so this someone is a friend / gang of friends. most of the time friends are mostly present in your life for enjoyment and fun, at times of need or so you will come to know each one's real face , hardly few of your friend might turn up to help you. There are very few friends who always stand beside you at times of sorrow or grief. A person is acquainted with many persons in their life . however, the closest ones become our friends . you may have a large friend circle in school or college, but you know you can only count on one or two people with whom you share true friendship.

There are essentially two types of friends , one is good friends the other are true friends or best friends . they are the ones with whom we have a special bond of love and affection . in other words , having true friends makes our life easier and full of happiness. Most importantly true friendships stands for a relationship free of any judgements in a true friendship, a person can be themselves completely without the fear of being judged . it makes you feel loved and accepted . this kind of freedom is what every human strives to have in their lives. In short, true friendship is what gives us reason to stay strong in life , having a loving family and all is okay but but you also need true friendship to be completely happy . some people do not even have families but they have friends who are like family only. Thus, we see having true friend means a lot to everyone .

A true friend never leaves your side in your bad times, your real friends will always motivate you and cheers for you. There is no doubt that best friends helps us in our difficulties and bad times of life . they always try to Save us in our dangers as well as offer timely advice . true friends are like the best assets of our life because they share our sorrow, sooth our pain and makes us feel happy.

CHAPTER THREE

WHY DO WE NEED A FRIEND..?

As of today, we live in a world growing at the fastest rate known to mankind . in this era where speed is the norm, it is hard to keep up with the world. Sometimes, you need something to hold on to, in order for you do not sleep and fall in life. And that is the time where you need a friend. Friends are the important part of our life .

The only person in the entire world you vcan expect to be brutally honest with you are this bunch of idiots they will never leave you in your bad times. They are the harsh counter part of your mirror that will never let you go wrong in your life. Your parents always trust your friends more than you. They constantly nitpick on you to be better and work harder just like some friends of yours does. While your friends are brutally about everything you do they would never do it at the cost of you falling apart. They will support your every endeavour and encourage you to be bold and confident.

They might have their reservations about certain things but that's only because they worry about you. Since, they know all your secrets, you have nothing to hide. Literally ; you are so comfortable with them that you don't even think twice before changing in front of them or doing out the stupidest thing ever . if you just want to talk your heart out, they are there. They will listen to you no matter how serious you are. For hours you can rant about your problems or excitedly fill them in honour new development in your life. Without judging you, without negativity , they will listen and be there for you , sometimes even without understanding.

If you have friends, you are not lonely. If you have friends you can ring up at any time of the day to just hang out with you, you can not be lonely. Friends help fill in the void . don't push them away when you are upset . pull them closer hug them tight and feel your sense of isolation slowly melt away automatically. Remember that time you broke your neighbors window while playing cricket and ran away without owning up or that time you went for that movie without your parents permission? You did it all with your closest friends . there are some things which you cant do with anyone and everyone .

Your friends are the most protective of you after your parents and siblings. They can say you are ugly or call your name many times in front of your crush. But if anyone else make fun of you they would skim them alive . no one can hurt you while they are there to guard you with all their life. Every emotional and physical stress is kept under strict surveillance and all bugs are debugged instantly .

do whatever you want to don in your life but one thing you should not do is to fight with your friend or to ignore them. We need a friend to survive in this world , where everything tends to change . friend is the only constant element that we can rely on, a friend is like our own personal warehouse where we dump our all worries and secrets. A warehouse, stocked with love and care , always!

One can always share happy moments with anyone , but when one is deeply sad about something he only searches for a person with whom he can share his trouble ,where he knows that he wont be judged at any cost and only. The major role is played by a friend.

Acceptance is what once looks for in the entire journey of life . acceptance by family , friends and society is the goal of every soul . where are acceptance by parents is something natural, but when it comes to friends, it is nothing less than a miracle . it is just a blessing, where one completely unknown person accepts you with all your faults and flaws.

Friendship is the hardest thing in the world to be explained in mere words . but still , I will try to explain or atleast give a brief idea of what a true and loyal friend means. You cannot expect everyone to behave the way you want them to behave. Still, there is atleast one of your mates whom you want to be with when you are suffering from low's in your life. Friends are that family whom we can choose to be with and therefore they are incredibly valued in each of our lives. Ofcourse , not every single day in our life can be perfect .

we all suffer from emotional pain or what you might know as depression . and to beat that thing you need a helping hand. And that helping hand which supports you when you are sad or when you need their help the most are known as friends and I don't specifically means friends who are with you at your play times or at school. Yes, they can be your helping hands but not everyone in this world is as lucky as I am having them at my help whenever I need them. If you don't have friends at all and you are depressed due to something you can always listen to music or read book at times.

Trust me they will never fail to meet your expectations . this proves that music, books etc can also be your friends if you want them too . I forgot to mention the most loyal creatures on this whole planet – dogs they also help you to get over some emotional pain to a great extent. A great friendship is irreplaceable it can inspire you to grow into a better version of yourself. If you have a such a nice friend , who motivates you , return the favour in some way or the other. A well said line by one of the scholar is "life is partly what we make it and partly what it is made by the friends we choose" so this means that you must always choose your friend circle with great sense of judgement.

Your close circle should not harm you in any way . it should be unique and specifically for you only. They help a lot when you are confused and a need a hand in decision making. Your close circle or the people whom you trust the most may forget what you said , but they will never forget how you made them feel. So , take special care of your actions and your words when you are addressing them, a real friend is the only person who walks in when the rest of the world walks out. So whenever you are in some sort of trouble just look around once and the people who are there to support you are your best mates .

this trick will help you to decide how much and in front of whom you can disclose your secrets its normal to argue or fight with your friends at times. But do not just let that fight that one fight change or defy the relation with your friend of several years. So just let go and say sorry to end the fight soon. Your good friends will always support and help you to achieve your dreams and ootcourse there is no life whatever materialistic thing you have, and have no one to share it with. So , friends make lifes definition successful.

CHAPTER FOUR

BEST FRIEND

A best friend is a person whom we can trust blindly. Best friends are on the top of friend list. We have lot of friends only for hi hello but only a person whom we can call at any time and any situation and talk for hours constantly are the best friends. best friend is the only person who understands your emotions very well other that anyone in this world. We do not hesitate to share anything from our best friend. They are the blessing of god to us. Let me tell about my best friends, I have three best friends pramod, anil and bittu.

PRAMOD...

We are friends from our kg class , we were best friends from that time , now our friendship is more than 16 yrs old. We know each other very well. We were in same school from our childhood time and we spent golden days of our life in delhi. He is from uttar Pradesh and he is very brave in nature having a brilliant mind, not more than me but he always supports me and give me direction to what to do next in my life. He is a very loyal person I trust him blindly.

He is a good cricket player too and now trying for a job in Indian army. I am his best friend too. As a person he is the only person whom I cant fight easily because he is very positive in nature and he have a lot of patience. We have a lot of memories together. He always supported me in my school fights. When we talk hours pass like minutes . we have also gone for tours together many times out of state and I like his company. His family also loves me.

ANIL.....

As he is from rajasthan and a rajput, his blood is also very hot and bravery is in his blood. Always ready to fight with anyone and supports me like nobody can. We are friends from last 13 years , we met in school in third standard and we were not good friends that time . we became friends after our 10thstandard . we came so close to each other . from going school in dtc bus without tickets to going in metro on a single ticket we shared a lot of memories together. We were caught manier times without ticket in bus checking but we loved travelling without tickets just for fun and save money. We go to tuitions together on bike without helmets and we enjoyed each others company.

We became best friends after 10thstandard . then we started to go gym in 11thclass . as he is my neighbor in delhi, it was my duty to wake him up in morning at 6 o clock and take him to the gym. He was my best gym partner till date. We spend a lot of time together as he was my childhood friend and neighbor also. So we know everything about each other, he is very much talented and flirty in nature , he also has good communication skills. He is also a good marketer that means he can sell anything.

As I am not in delhi now a days so my family calls him for any work. He is also like my family member not just for me but my family also. Some people exists in life who can never ask whether you are wrong or right , they just support you , he is one of them. I love him a lot. He is a loyal friend and he doesnot have any bad habits. He asks me before taking any major decisions. Once upon a time we were enemies. But as time passed we became brothers for life . he is always ready to fight with anyone for me and he has also done it for manier tims. I love him a lot and it is my dream to dance a lot in his in his wedding.

BITTU....

Our friendship is not very old but not always old is gold . he is the best gift of god to me in my life after my family. He is the one and only whom I share my everything. He is from Jamshedpur and we met in college , as we didn't knew each other from years. We met in college freshers party , from going college together on motor cycle to sharing clothes our friendship converted to brotherhood. He is the one who always supports me , we faced a lot of problems in our life and he is the one who is always there .

we spend a lot of time together as he is my first friend in Jamshedpur we always used to roam with each other at any time, morning, noon, evening and night. My family and his family treats each other as a family member. We have a lot of memories together , I want to share some of the memories like it was around three years back he was suffering from stomach pain and doctors told that he is having a stone in his gall bladder which should be removed by surgery immediately and he was admitted to hospital and then while he was in hospital and unconscious , I go to hospital to meet him daily and take his girl friend also along with me to meet her.

it was the first time when we were connected emotionally so much. And after he was discharged from hospital doctors suggested him 7 days bed rest. But on third day he told me that he want to eat noodles then we went and after coming back we both were scolded a lot by his parents. After that we became very good friends , he once posted that he does not have any brother so he wants me as his brother in his life. He is a car lover, he loves to be on top and in fame. He want popularity and politics too. Politics because to be popular, we also fight a lot with each other , he loves to be in videos and photographs.

After fights he is the one who always convince me. As time passed we came closer and our friendship became more stronger and I always share my everything with him because he is the only person who knows me well and sometimes he knows everything even when I don't say a word , that's the power of our friendship. We went on college tour to dehradoon,mussorie, and had a lot of fun . we had a fight there . he can do anything for me, there are some people in our life whom we can trust blindly he is one of them , I ask once before taking any decisions in my life , so he is the one who knows everything about me, there are a lot of memories of us together . we once bunked our college and went to a restaurant and one of our friend posted on instagram with caption"bunk time" .

and then we were caught by college authorities. I want bittu with me for the rest of my life with me. The most important incident in our life which I want to share is that – it was a year ago when we were at cyber café and taking printouts of our MAT exam admit cards which was on the very next day, and after taking print out he give that to me to take along with me to the college on the next day. On the next morning I was getting ready for the college , I called him but the phone was not reachable then I ignored , after a hour when I was getting late for the exam and didn't came to pick me up, I was little tensed but then I called him but the phone was still not reachable , I did not understand what was happening at that time. I told my father that he is not yet came , my father told me that whether there was some problem you go to college he will meet you there and I went to college and exam was yet to start but did not came.

I thought that something was not good. After some time he entered into examination hall with 5 policemen having guns and he was crying . we both started crying after seeing each other and he told me that take care of my family and .... , I will be going to jail and come after 3-4 months and he told me that he has been trapped in a false case . we both cried for 3 hours and it was worst day. After the exam when he was going I did not understand what to do. Police take him to the police jeep and I followed the jeep to the police station and cried a lot. The person who swipes my tears was in pain. It hurt me a lot. Then on the next day he has been taken to central jail and case hss been filed on him .

I went to jail to meet him on regular intervals . then after three months he was out of that. And I just wanted to meet him. He when came out of jail did not told anyone but somehow I managed to know that he was outside and I went to his home but he was not there and then I started crying and then his parents told me that on that day he was going to bihar and they called him and told that I want to talk to him then I talked to him and went to station and meet him. I was very happy to meet him after a very big Interval of time.

Conclusion

There should be a friend in life whom we can trust blindly and to whom we can share all of our secrets. friends are very important in our life and friends can help you overcoming many obstacles of life.